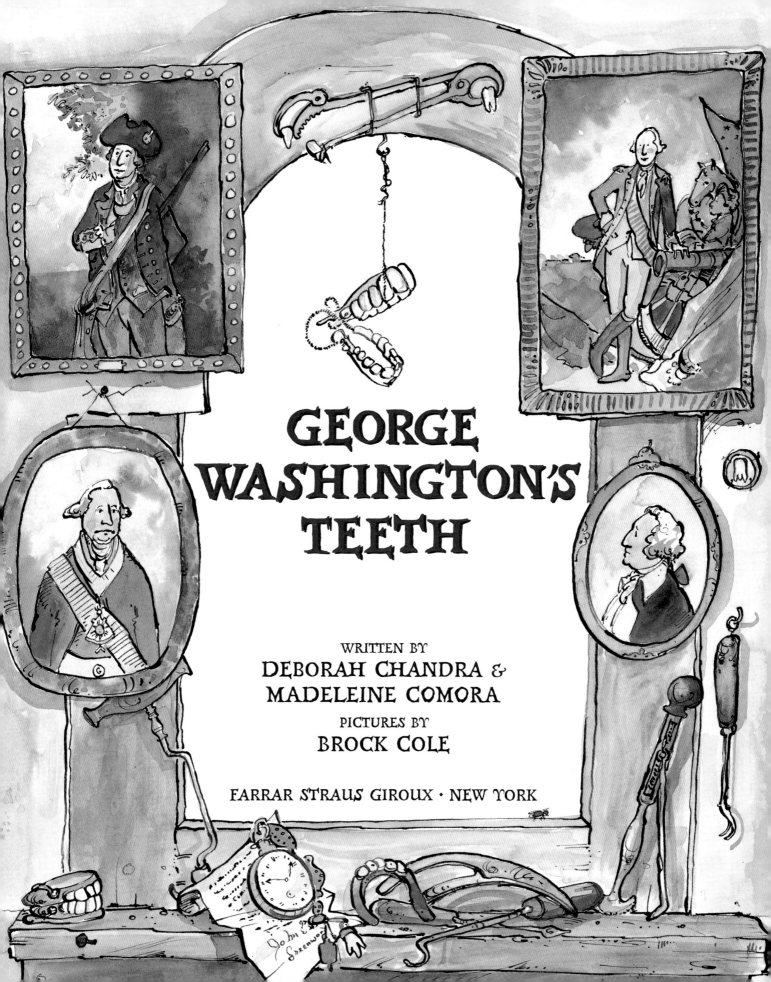

GEORGE WASHINGTON'S TEETH

WRITTEN BY
DEBORAH CHANDRA &
MADELEINE COMORA
PICTURES BY
BROCK COLE

FARRAR STRAUS GIROUX · NEW YORK

For Sam and Nathan and Sharie

with love

D.C.

For my father, Emanuel M. Comora, D.M.D., who gave me the idea

M.C.

For Donald F. Cole, D.D.S.

B.C.

All of his life, George Washington had problems with his teeth and worked hard to save them. This story is based on what really happened to George and his teeth.

The Revolutionary War
George hoped would soon be won,
But another battle with his teeth
Had only just begun . . .

George Washington rushed into town,
The dentist heard his shout.

"Hold still," he said, then gave a yank—
A rotten tooth popped out!

All that night George tossed and moaned,
Another tooth was sore.

But at the dawn he saddled up
And galloped off to war.

George reached New York as British ships
Invaded every port.

Preparing for a fierce attack,
His soldiers built a fort.

Inside he rubbed his swollen gums
With soothing oil of myrrh,
Until a sentinel cried out,
"Here come the British, sir!"

Charging on the field, George thought,
"There's something in my mouth."
He spat into his handkerchief,
Another tooth came out!

"This can't be happening," George gasped.
"What if someone should see?
If word got out I'm losing teeth,
My men would laugh at me."

While no one looked, he wrote a note
His dentist would receive.
"Please come," it said, "I'll need your help
When I get home on leave."

Back at home George lost more teeth
Till he had only *ten*.
"Oh, Martha dear," George cried,
"I fear I'll never eat again!"

She fed him mush and pickled tripe,
But when guests came to dine,

He sneaked one of his favorite nuts.

Then he had only *nine*.

George crossed the icy Delaware
With nine teeth in his mouth.

In that cold and pitchy dark,
Two more teeth came out!

Snow fell on George at Valley Forge,
His blue coat hung in tatters.
By then he'd only *seven* teeth
That couldn't even chatter!

Yet bravely George led forth his men,
Coat and pigtail flying.
While cannons boomed he held his jaw
And groaned, "I think I'm dying!"

The Redcoats fled—George won the war!
When he returned alive,

Martha checked for seven teeth
But counted only *five*.

He hid the evening of her ball,
Ashamed his friends would see.
That night the dentist came again—
George lost *another three*!

Poor George had *two* teeth in his mouth
The day the votes came in.
The people had a President,
But one afraid to grin.

A portrait artist came to George.
He said, "I know a trick!
I'll pad your mouth with cotton balls
To puff your sunken lips."

George stood up to have a look—
He fell back on his fanny.
"It doesn't look like me!" he roared.
"It looks like Martha's granny!"

He yanked the cotton from his mouth,
Then gasped, "What have I done?"
The cotton held a rotten tooth.
Now George had only *one*!

George still had that tooth the night
A knock came at the door.
"I've brought false teeth," the dentist called,
"Teeth that won't get sore!"

George put them in, but when he smiled,
Springs snapped against his tongue.

Out flew those teeth—"Aagh!" George shrieked.
"They've knocked out my *last one*!"

"Oh no," George moaned, "I'm toofless!"
He kept his mouth shut tight.

He couldn't sleep. He paced the floor,
And prayed with all his might.

"If only I had teeth," thought George.
He pondered what to do.

"Aha!" he cried. "All my old teeth
Might help make something new!"

He searched Mount Vernon's bedchambers,

The pantry, parlors, halls,

Through shelves, desk drawers, and the musty floor

Of every horse's stall.

George found no teeth. "Alas, they're gone."
A great sob shook his shoulders.

Through tears he peered in one last chest,
Leaped up and yelled . . . "My molars!"

With plaster and those teeth he found,
George poured a sample mold
That showed the dentist how to make
False teeth George hoped would hold.

The dentist took strong hippo tusk
And carved a set to size—
Each tooth secured with screws of gold
That lit up George's eyes!

Can you guess the story's end?
Those new teeth fit just right.

And round the ballroom with his friends
George danced all through the night!

Important events in George Washington's life

1732

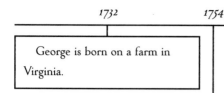

George is born on a farm in Virginia.

1754

George is twenty-two. He has already lost two teeth. The others are black and rotted.

1755

While serving in the French and Indian War, George sends for dental supplies: toothbrushes, tooth powders, sponges, scrapers, tincture of myrrh. He invites a dentist to his army headquarters, although he fears the British will find out and poke fun at his dental difficulties, as they have in the past.

1756

George's first tooth is extracted. Almost every year from here on, he loses more teeth.

1776

George is forty-four. He and his men cross the Delaware River. Charles Willson Peale paints another portrait of George—this one shows a scar on his left cheek from an abscessed tooth.

Old root fragments embedded in George's gums are causing him great pain.

1781

George wears some false teeth that are held in place by wires half hitched around his remaining teeth.

He sends a letter to Dr. Baker: "A day or two ago I requested Colonel Harrison to apply to you for a pair of pincers to fasten the wire of my teeth.—I hope you furnished him with them.—I now wish you would send me one of your scrapers as my teeth stand in need of cleaning." The letter is intercepted by the British and never reaches Dr. Baker.

1782

George remembers he has saved some teeth. He writes a letter to his cousin Lund: "In a drawer in the Locker of the Desk which stands in my study you will find two small teeth, which I beg you to wrap up carefully and send inclosed in your next Letter to me."

—*from his own letters, diaries, and accounts*

1772 1773 1774 1775

George is forty. He travels to Williamsburg to have a tooth extracted by his dentist, Dr. John Baker.

His first portrait is painted by Charles Willson Peale.

George often eats pickled tripe, which is soft and doesn't hurt his teeth. In a letter to a London merchant he writes: "Mrs. Washington joins me in warm thanks to you for your considerate present of two large stone jars of pickled tripe. I must ask you to arrange for four similar jars . . . Dental infirmity impels me caring for this necessary item in our domestic comissariat."

George orders Jordan almonds and other favorite candied confections, even though they are hard on his teeth and difficult to eat.

The American Revolutionary War begins.

George is elected General and Commander in Chief of the Continental Army.

1783 1785 1786 1787

The American Revolutionary War ends.

Letter to Dr. Baker: "I shall be obliged for some of the plaster of Paris . . . with which you take the model of the mouth for your false teeth—and directions how to mix and make use of it—When you have done this I can then give you back a model as will enable you to furnish me with what I want."

Letter to a watchmaker who makes small instruments: "I pray you send me a small file or two, one of which to be very thin, so much so as to pass between the Teeth if occasion shall require it—another one round."

George mixes plaster of Paris and makes a model with teeth he has saved. His dentist uses the model to make George's false teeth.

George sends a letter to Lieutenant Colonel William S. Smith inquiring about the dentist Dr. Jean Pierre Le Meyeur, "of whose skill much has been said . . . Having some teeth which give me a great deal of pain, and of which I wish to be eased . . . and gums which might be relieved by a man of skill." He then crosses out the words "give me a great deal of pain" and writes instead "are very troublesome to me at times."

Dr. Le Meyeur, his new dentist, pays many visits to Mount Vernon.

George often writes to Dr. Le Meyeur. The letters are hand-delivered to keep his dental problems a secret.

George suffers from infections caused by his remaining teeth and the old root fragments.

Diary entry: "Seized with an ague before six o'clock this morning after having labored under a fever all night."

Diary entry: "A rheumatic complaint which has followed me more than six months, is frequently so bad that it is sometimes with difficulty I can raise my hand to my head, or turn myself in bed."

1788

George is frequently in bed with more infections.

1789

George is elected President. He has two teeth left in his mouth: the lower right first molar and the lower left bicuspid, or premolar.

His new dentist, Dr. John Greenwood, removes the lower right first molar.

George's first full set of false teeth is made by Dr. Greenwood out of hippopotamus ivory and eight human teeth held in place with gold screw rivets. The base is coated with flesh-tinted sealing wax to give a natural appearance.

1790

Diary entry: "At home all day—not well. Still indisposed with an aching tooth and swelled and inflamed gum."

George sometimes wears an old set of dentures which has a base of lead alloy coated with beeswax. The dentures are held together with springs of coiled steel so powerful that George's jaws have to work hard at keeping the upper and lower parts together.

A traveler writes of George: "His mouth was like no other I ever saw; the lips firm and the under jaw seemed to grasp the upper with force, as if the muscles were in full actions when he sat still."

1791.

George gets another set of false teeth from Dr. Greenwood. He sends them back for repairs, anxious that they be fixed before Congress reopens.

George gives a large dinner party. Later, one guest writes: "The President seemed to bear in his countenance a settled aspect of melancholy . . . At every interval of eating and drinking he played on the table with a fork or a knife like a drumstick."

1797

George suffers from deafness caused by the unnatural motion of the lower jaw when he wears his dentures. He is embarrassed to speak in public because of the shape of his face and the hollow and indistinct quality of his voice caused by the artificial teeth.

He sends his false teeth to Dr. Greenwood for changes and switches to an old set which causes his lips to bulge out.

Letter to his dentist: "Send with the teeth, springs about a foot in length, but not cut; and about double that length of a tough gold wire, of the size you see with the teeth, for fastening the springs."

Although George's hands are large, he uses them for the delicate task of coiling gold wire into springs.

1798

George is sixty-six. He asks Dr. Greenwood to make more changes to his false teeth and gives him instructions for a custom fit.

George's last full set of false teeth is made. The palate is swaged from a sheet of gold. Riveted to it with gold pins are teeth carved from hippopotamus ivory. Two sections of teeth, attached to the upper base with wooden dowels, are replaceable. The lower denture is carved from a single block of ivory and coated with flesh-tinted sealing wax. The dentures are held together by fine-coiled springs made of gold wire. Strong facial muscles are required to hold the set in place.

George complains that his false teeth have become discolored. Dr. Greenwood tells him that the stains are caused "either by your soaking them in port wine or your drinking it." He advises George to "take them out after dinner and put them in clear water . . . or clean them with a brush and some chalk scraped fine."

George is sixty-two. He can't chew with his false teeth and suffers from indigestion and bad temper. He doesn't like to remove his false teeth at the dinner table as most people do. He is sad at dinner and keeps his mouth closed.

William Williams paints his portrait.

George is sixty-four. His last tooth is giving him trouble. Still, he hates the thought of parting with it. Dr. Greenwood makes a large opening in George's lower denture to allow his last tooth to pass through. It stops his lower denture from moving outward from the force of the springs, but as a result, the tooth becomes loose and aches and the surrounding gums swell up.

The size of George's denture, together with the action of the muscles to keep it in place, makes him look as if he is pouting.

George poses for Gilbert Stuart, who later paints many portraits based on this sitting. He pads

George's lips and cheeks with cotton because his face is sunken from his short dentures. The padding makes him look soft and grandmotherly.

George's last tooth is removed by Dr. Greenwood, who later encases it in gold and wears it on his watch chain.

George dies at Mount Vernon at the age of sixty-seven. It is believed that a chronic, untreated infection from the old root fragments in his gums contributed to his death.

After his death, Charles de St. Mémin does an etching based on a life mask of George.

Throughout his life George had many sets of false teeth made from different materials: hippopotamus, walrus, and elephant ivory, and cow, elk, and human teeth. But he never had a set of wooden teeth. The very last denture Dr. Greenwood made for him was a partial set, which George was wearing when he died.

Final Note: George's account books show that between the years 1772 and 1792 the medical bills for himself, his family, and around two hundred slaves amounted to $100 per year. By comparison, George's dental bills were $1,000 per year.

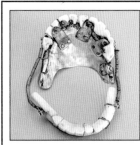 

Two views of George's last set of dentures made by Dr. Greenwood. The teeth are carved from hippopotamus ivory, the palate swaged from a sheet of gold, and the springs made of coiled gold wire.

TIME LINE SOURCES:

Blanton, Wyndham B. *Washington's Medical Knowledge and Its Sources.* Annals of Medical History, vol. 5. New York: P. B. Hoeber, 1933. Pp. 55–56.

Eisen, Gustavus A. *Portraits of Washington.* Vol. 2. New York: R. Hamilton & Associates, 1932.

Fitzpatrick, John C., ed. *Diaries of George Washington, 1748–1799.* 4 vols. Boston and New York: Houghton Mifflin, 1925.

Fitzpatrick, John C. *George Washington Himself: A Common-Sense Biography Written from His Manuscripts.* Indianapolis: Bobbs-Merrill, 1933.

———. *The Writings of George Washington from the Original Manuscript Sources, 1748–1799.* Washington, D.C.: U.S. Government Printing Office, 1931. Vols. 1, 3, 4, 22, 25, 26, 27, 28, 29, 31, 35, 36.

Ford, Paul Leicester. *The True George Washington.* Philadelphia: J. B. Lippincott, 1900. P. 40.

Glenner, Richard A., Audrey B. Davis, and Stanley B. Burns. *The American Dentist: A Pictorial History with a Presentation of Early Dental Photography in America.* Montana: Pictorial Histories, 1900. P. 50.

Lufkin, Arthur Ward. *A History of Dentistry.* Philadelphia: Lea & Febiger, 1948. Pp. 171, 178.

Ring, Malvin E. *Dentistry: An Illustrated History.* New York: Abrams, 1985. Pp. 192–93, 211.

Weinberger, Bernhard Wolf. *An Introduction to the History of Dentistry in America: Washington's Need for Medical and Dental Care.* St. Louis: C. V. Mosby, 1948. Pp. 298, 300, 307–8, 310, 318, 321, 330–31.

Woodforde, John. *The Strange Story of False Teeth.* London: Routledge & Kegan Paul, 1968. Pp. 98, 100, 102.

ART SOURCES:

George Washington in the Uniform of a British Colonial Colonel, 1772, by Charles Willson Peale, American (1741–1827). Oil on canvas, 50½ x 41½ in. Washington-Custis-Lee Collection, Washington and Lee University, Lexington, Virginia. Reprinted with permission.

George Washington, 1776, by Charles Willson Peale, American (1741–1827). Oil on canvas, 44⅛ x 38½ in. Brooklyn Museum of Art, Dick S. Ramsay Fund, 34.1178. Reprinted with permission.

George Washington, 1794, by William Joseph Williams, American (1759–1823). Pastel on paper, 28 x 22 in. Collection of Alexandria-Washington Masonic Lodge No. 22. Reprinted with permission.

George Washington, 1810, by Gilbert Stuart, American (1755–1828). Oil on panel, 26 x 21⅝ in. Museum of Fine Arts, Boston, Bequest of George Nixon Black, 29.788. Reprinted with permission.

George Washington, 1800, by Charles de St. Mémin, American (1770–1852). Engraving, ⅝ x ⁷⁄₁₆ in. In the collection of the Corcoran Gallery of Art (75.16, folio 50L). Reprinted with permission.

Photographs of George Washington's dentures are from the National Museum of American History at the Smithsonian Institution, Washington, D.C. Reprinted with permission.

The authors wish to acknowledge the following for their help: Mount Vernon Ladies' Association, Mount Vernon; National Portrait Gallery, Smithsonian; The Papers of George Washington Project, University of Virginia.

Library of Congress Cataloging-in-Publication Data

Chandra, Deborah.
    George Washington's teeth / written by Deborah Chandra and Madeleine Comora ;
pictures by Brock Cole.
       p.   cm.
    Summary: A rollicking rhyme portrays George Washington's lifelong struggle with bad
teeth. A timeline taken from diary entries and other nonfiction sources follows.
    ISBN 0-374-32534-0
    1. Washington, George, 1732–1799—Health—Anecdotes—Juvenile literature. 2. Tooth
loss—United States—Anecdotes—Juvenile literature. [1. Washington, George, 1732–1799.
2. Presidents. 3. Teeth. 4. Diaries.] I. Comora, Madeleine. II. Cole, Brock, ill. III. Title.

E312.66.C48 2003
973.4'1'092—dc21

                                                                              2002025086